Dating Down...
And Those of US Who Do It

A Learning WORKBOOK with funstuff

CAROLE H. FIELD, M.A., M.F.T
Author and Psychotherapist

ISBN: 1-4392-4791-9
ISBN-13: 9781439247914

Visit www.booksurge.com to order additional copies.

TABLE OF CONTENTS

PART 1
FORWARD

Dear Reader,

Most of you already have the main text, *Dating Down... and Those of Us Who Do It*. In it, it suggests that you read each story and then attend to the story's analysis, the red flags.

In terms of this workbook, one of two suggestions is in order. 1. Read the entire main text and then begin the work in the workbook, or, 2. After each story and red flag in the main text, work on the corresponding chapters in this workbook. Either way is fine.

Also, there are other basic exercises in this workbook that do not directly correspond to the main text. You can enjoy and work on them at any time. They shall also prove helpful in this process. And, as you shall discover, there are some pieces in this workbook just to read and not work on. Yet, everything will be contributing to your enhanced growth in this arena.

Also, if you do not have sufficient space in the provided pages, definitely add your own paper. It is strongly suggested you begin by having your own extra paper. And remember, nobody is grading you or judging your responses. This is your book – not your best friend's, boyfriend's, teacher's, mother's, etc... No grading.

Make this your personal learning experience. Be willing to verbally share the experience with your friends but you do not have to physically show them your special writing, drawing, responses, and so forth.

Also, as friendly and fun as this workbook appears, there will be much processing, so take it slow. It will probably take you many weeks. You are not on some timed deadline. Feel free to jump around the workbook and make changes to your answers. That is all fine. No grading.

Oh – and one last note! As always, as you plough through the workbook (and your life), keep in mind four key musts:

- Be as honest as you possibly can.
- Be as responsible as you possibly can.
- When in doubt, opt for kindness.
- Have a helluva time!

I am with you on your journey, our journey, everyone's inspired discovery.

~ Carole

PART 2
FROM: WELCOME TO THE TURBULENT WORLD OF DATING DOWN – THE INTRODUCTION OF THE MAIN TEXT

1. Why, at this time in your life, did you gravitate to *Dating Down… and Those of US Who Do It* ? You had thousands of books from which to choose. Although a good choice, still, why this book?

2. A number of introductory concepts were defined and elaborated upon in the book's introduction. What was the most meaningful concept you took away from the introduction?

3. Birthdays and holidays are important to most people. Isabella's birthday party was expressed. What was your feeling about the event?

4. A) The definition of dating down and the five constants of a downdatee are explained in this introduction.

Study each constant (listed below) and fill in one event or person the particular constant brings to mind for you. They might all be the same event or person. In the blanks provided, write down the first person or event who comes to mind. If you are really stuck, place a Ø.
Constant #1 –

The female frequently takes on full responsibility for the male's unhealthy, unproductive, or harmful behavior.
This reminds me of_____.
Constant #2 –

The male in this relationship exhibits a stubborn resistance to change his maladaptive behavior.
This reminds me of_____.

Constant #3 –

The female endures unmet needs for months or even years.
This reminds me of_____.

Constant #4 –

The discrepancy or mismatch in this couple is markedly apparent by the objective and knowledgeable observer.
This reminds me of_____.

Constant #5 –

And the beat goes on...as the downdater endures frustration, accepts blame, and blindly tolerates his resistance of necessary change.

This reminds me of_____.

4. B) Who is on the above list the most? What do you wish to say about this person (or event)?

5. This book was filled with illustrative stories and much information in the red flags. How do you now define dating down in your own words?

6. Think back to before you read this book. How would you have defined dating down then (if at all)?

7. It might be a good idea to call a friend this week and discuss your definitions of dating down. How do they compare or contrast?

8. What was your favorite of the eight stories?

9. With what story did you most identify?

10. Which of the story's red flags meant the most to you in your life? Why?

PART 3
QUESTIONS ABOUT THE "FIVE CONSTANTS" IN THE INTRODUCTION

In the Introduction of *Dating Down and Those of Us Who Do It*, five constants are listed which are the requirements for a relationship to be a downdating relationship.

Answer the following multiple-choice questions to the best of your ability. (Remember – nobody is grading this questionnaire.)

1. The female frequently takes on full responsibility for the males' unhealthy, unproductive or harmful behavior.

Question: Which is the most true?

A. This is not a dating down relationship if the male promises to change in the future after he moves his residence, he gets a job change, his kids grow up, etc...

B. This is not a dating down relationship if the female takes on approximately 80% of the responsibilities – not 100%.

C. This is not a dating down relationship if the man has suddenly been taken ill and the female must step up to the plate, more than usual.

D. This is not a dating down relationship if the male is very responsible but is harmful to the female's self-esteem.

2. The male in this relationship exhibits a stubborn resistance to charge his maladaptive behavior.

Question: Dating down...

A. Is almost always about someone being resistant.
B. Is only about staying in a relationship with a resistant significant other.
C. Has nothing to do with resistance, really. Resistance is usually a fascinating challenge where everyone learns, grows, and develops emotional muscles.
D. Is not really about maladaptive or unhealthy behavior.

3. The female endures unmet needs for months or even years.

Circle the best letter:

A. Enduring unmet needs is no big deal.
B. Enduring unmet needs is what most people require to become stronger.
C. Unmet needs for many months is no problem. Unmet needs for years is only where the problem starts.
D. Unmet needs, to a major degree, incurs physical problems.

4. The discrepancy or mismatch in this couple is markedly apparent by the objective and knowledgeable observer.

Circle the best letter:

A. Every relationship has a dating down element to it and therefore every relationship is a dating down relationship.

B. Relationships are only dating down relationships when they are defined as such by someone outside the couple.
C. Relationships can never be judged by anyone else.
D. Thermometers and barometers, at least, have some standard of concrete objectivity.

5. And the beat goes on...as the downdater endures frustration, accepts blame, and blindly tolerates his resistance to necessary change.

<u>Circle the best letter:</u>

A. Dating down is a one-time / one day only problem.
B. Enduring frustration always implies downdating.
C. Constant blame is no big deal unless you are a weak personality.
D. Frustration and blame on a regular basis can make almost anyone deeply upset.

6. A. NOW – go back with another colored pen or pencil and circle the letters which your significant other might circle.

Ask yourself – are the differences here invisible, small, medium, or gy-normous?

B. Write about these differences and how they affect your personal feelings.

C. Write about your discussing these differences with him – or why you won't. You will learn a lot in doing this even thought "a lot" is not good English.

PART 4
REMINDER:

Dating Down is not about helping someone through a difficult period. You must / we must help each other through difficult periods.

Also keep in mind, all relationships have elements that need to be changed.

Difficult periods and weak elements do not equal dating down.

Reminder.

PART 5
CHAPTER 1 – COULD IT BE ICESKATE INTRODUCTIONS?

Depiction of a downdatee who: repeatedly commits personal or social fraudulence.
Protagonist: Mariska

1. Mariska and her Grandmama Henrietta experienced an unspoken closeness. Name one person in your life with whom you might share an unspoken closeness.

_____

Oddly, despite the closeness, what are the pitfalls in this closeness or in this relationship?

2. The first time you met a significant other, who approached whom? How did that particular approach work out, and why?

3. What was your first clue that something about Mariska's significant other was untrue, fraudulent?

4. This story illuminated the downdatee that repeatedly commits fraudulence. When did you fall into a fraudulent relationship (even to a small degree. Does not have to have been with a love interest)? What red flags were you missing?

5. Bernice entered Mariska's life quite surprisingly. How would you have communicated with her that afternoon?

6. Much was discussed and explained in the red flags. Which explanation stood out the most for you, and why?

7. If you were a "Heavenly Messenger" (work with me here), and you had to give Mariska a message after she broke up with Neil, what would you have told her?

8. Mariska was very reluctant to date after she stopped seeing Neil. How are you after you break up with someone? What is your normal "breather time" and do you want to change your "breather time" or not?

PART 6
CHAPTER 2 – THE THREE MARIAS

Depiction of a downdater who: Is a convicted or non-convicted career criminal or recidivist.
Protagonist: Maria

1. The word empathy is defined as, "Identification with and understanding of another's situation, feelings and motives." It is often confused with sympathy. Sympathy is defined as, "A feeling or expression of pity or sorrow for the distress of another." So, empathy is about understanding whereas sympathy is about pity.

What follows is going to be an exercise in empathy training. It works, and it is fun.

A. In view of Maria in the story, "The Three Marias", from what you learned about her, fill in the following:

What do you suppose Maria's favorite of the following might be?
    Music:
    Food:
    Style of Dress:
    Holiday:
    Magazine:
    Pet:
    Place to travel:
    Political leanings:
    Game:

Book:
Pastime:
Sport:
Dance form:
Subject in school:
Car:
(If you are not sure at all, just place a question mark.)

B. Now, do this again for yourself.
Your name_____
Music:
Food:
Style of dress:
Holiday:
Magazine:
Pet:
Place to travel:
Political leanings:
Game:
Book:
Pastime:
Sport:
Dance form:
Subject in school:
Car:

C. Now, do this again in relation to someone you do not know well (example – a neighbor, a co-worker, a substitute teacher, a family acquaintance, a nearby clerk in a store, anyone) Just try it.

Name (or position in your life) _____

Music:

Food:

Style of dress:

Holiday:

Magazine:

Pet:

Place to travel:

Political leanings:

Game:

Book:

Pastime:

Sport:

Dance form:

Subject in school:

Car:

D. Now, try the same exercise with your significant other / spouse / crush / old boyfriend, etc...

His name_____

Music:

Food:

Style of dress:

Holiday:

Magazine:

Pet:

Place to travel:

Political leanings:

Game:

Book:

Pastime:

Sport:

Dance form:

Subject in school:

Car:

E. Do this before you see your significant other. Then, present it to him. Ask him to fill in where you were correct or incorrect. Then, ask yourself and him why you came up with these particular empathic projections. If you were correct, congratulations. If you were way off, you might want to question if your empathic radar needs some practice, or if he is giving you "confusing vibes."

This easy exercise in empathy training is not a bad orientation to practice with family members and all future significant others.

2. Sometimes we have to do things we do not want to do, or, find ourselves in less than optimal situations. Here comes a big "What If."

What if you had to spend an evening with Tony, knowing full well of his illegal lifestyle. Say, he did not know you knew about him, but you did. You had to design the date (stay safe now). What would this date look like, where would you go, with whom, and so forth...?

3. Do you remember an evening or an activity that was less than wonderful? How did you handle it?

4. At what point do you think Maria became aware of Tony's leanings and aware she was clearly, and unsafely, dating down?

5. Can you remember a time when you knew your significant other was not there for your highest good? Write about exactly how you felt when you "got it." How much denial did you continue to employ?

PART 7
QUESTION

Are you involved with a

circle of people who are the

best for your highest self?

PART 8
TAKIN' A BREAK

Okay, let's take a working break for a moment.

On this page, please glue a photo or photos or your own drawing of someone who inspires you and is there for your highest good.

On the next page, place a photo(s) or drawing of someone who is not there for your highest good. Label the pictures. Under the second group of photos, also write one sentence why this person(s) is not there for your highest good.

TAKE A LOOK

And now, I am happy to show you some family / friend / or other entity photos who have always been there for my highest good. Enjoy.

CHAPTER 3 – TO CALL UPON MY GOD

Depiction of downdatee who: has a highly addictive personality, yet denounces any Twelve Step or therapeutic support.

Protagonist: Rachel

1. This downdatee is defined as, basically, an addict who will not seek help for his addiction.

Do you know anyone in your life like this? What is your relationship to him? How has he affected your life? Your friends? Your family?

How would life be different if he was not involved in his addiction? (Remember readers, whenever I wrote "he" it does not have to be a significant other, and it could also mean "she").

2. The understanding of alcoholism and addiction have come a rather long way since the 1930s. What do you think life would be like without Alcoholics Anonymous, psychotherapists who understand addiction, drug and alcohol counselors, etc.?

3. Let's pretend dating down is as serious as alcoholism.
Where are you in your dating down evolution?

    A. Similar to an alcoholic before 1930 who was rendered fairly clueless? _____

    B. Someone with a glimpse of understanding of the problem?

    _____

    C. Someone who has read the main text and has more of an understanding?

    _____

    D. Someone who has started a dating down discussion group and who fully intends to never again traverse that road?

    _____

    E. Other:

4. Where do you want to be in your evolution regarding this behavior?

    In three months: _____
    _____

    In six months: _____

    _____

    In two years: _____

    _____

5. On Rachel's first date with Rob she asked him to dinner. What do you think about having someone to dinner on a first date?

Do you have "rules" regarding first dates?

6. Pretend you were invited to that dinner. Draw where everyone was probably seated (you, Rachel, Rob, Philip, Jacob, their two friends)

7. From that dinner alone, what would you have learned from Rachel and Rob?

8. If you were also in the room when Rob poured a large, fourth glass of wine and you _had_ to say something, what would you have said?

9. Was there a time in your life when you wanted to say something to someone at a dinner, a party, or with a group

of other folks, but did not? How did you feel not expressing yourself? What did you get out of it / not get out of it? How do you wish to change that behavior in the future?

10. How does Rachel's religion benefit her life? If possible, how might it hinder her growth?

11. Rachel's best friend was a Palestinian woman in Israel. Rachel seemed to turn to her when she was really distraught and requiring the closeness of a galfriend. When do you do that? When not? What is best for you – to ramp this up a little, or to pull back?

12. "Angel time" again. You are guardian angel _____
_____ (fill in your name). Give Rachel a one-line message of hope.

_____

Now, give one to yourself.

_____

PART 11
A LIST

1. A) List five people with whom you are very close –

   1. _____

   2. _____

   3. _____

   4. _____

   5. _____

B) How would you assess all of their love relationships?

C) How does their relationship to their significant other affect you?

PART 12
DRAWING TIME

Take out some crayons or colored pencils. If you do not have any, pens or plain pencils will work just fine. Remember, you are not being graded. (You will definitely need your own paper for this part.)

A. Draw dinnertime as it typically looked in your childhood (the table, the food, the kitchen, people in the scene, etc. ...)

B. Draw dinnertime with a significant other (or downdatee), or, just dinnertime today.

C. Write how they compare.

D. Draw how you would like a "perfect" dinnertime to be today.

PART 13
TAKE ANOTHER LOOK

And now, for another work break. Here are some photographs of, yet, more people "and entities" in my life who have been supportive.

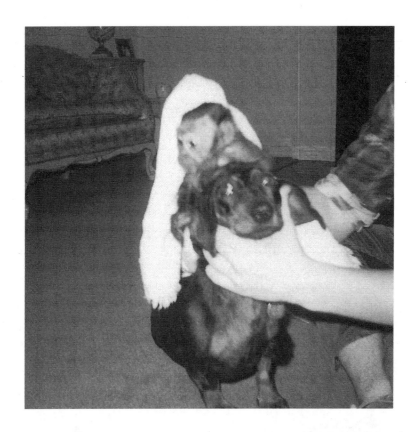

PART 14
CHAPTER 4 – DRUGS AND HUGS

Depiction of a downdatee who: has no conscience about bringing the female's body and/or mind directly into an illegal and dangerous lifestyle.
Protagonist: Lynda

1. What was your general sense of Lynda? Did you think she was fairly well adjusted, not at all adjusted, etc....

2. What is your feeling around someone who dances topless? Circle the closest answer to your feelings and sensibilities.
   A. It's great. It should be more readily available and less underground.
   B. It is usually a tacky show with untalented "performers."
   C. I have no idea because I've never been to one of those clubs.
   D. I think it is disgusting – one step away from prostitution.
   E. A good way to earn a living.
   F. It celebrates the beautiful female form.
   G. Everything is relative. It has its upside.

3. Do you have friends who are "exotic performers" or are in other careers whereby you might disapprove? Yes_____ No _____

    A. If you do, how do you handle talking about their "career"?

    B. How do you generally handle communication of topics where you might not approve?

4. A. What kind of relationship does it look like Lynda had with her mom as a child?

    B. What kind of relationship does she have with her mother today?

    C. What kind of relationship did you have with your mother as a child?

D. What about as an adult?

E. What kind of relationship did you have with your dad as a child?

F. What about as an adult?

G. How do you imagine Lynda's relationship with her mom as a child might have contributed to her dating down a drug addict?

5. A. Lynda has a totally different relationship to her mom now, than she did as a child. Do you think this will help her in the future? Why?

B. How do you think your relationship to your mother as a child contributes to your significant other choices today?

C. How do you think your relationship to your father as a child contributes to your significant other choices today?

6. A. Place Lynda and one of the other women we have used so far in this workbook (Mariska, Maria, Rachel) in a room together. Write a little dialogue of them discussing their boyfriends (at any point in their stories). Remember – you are not being graded and nobody is seeing this workbook. Just have fun. And, if you want to write an entire one-act play between these two characters, the sky is the limit.

B. Now – place Jason, Lynda's significant other, and the significant other of the other woman you have chosen, in a dialogue. How do these two men relate? Let your imagination run wild.

C. How were the two conversations different? What can you learn from this difference?

7. On the last red flag of Lynda's story, *Drugs and Hugs*, the question is asked, "Where is Lynda in Jason's life?"

Think of a time when you (or a friend) were connected to a downdatee. Where were you in his life? What did you really mean to him based on how he treated you and his behavior (not his words)?

PART 15
A NON-RHYMING POEM FOR YOU

I came across a photograph today.
Grandma was wearing a summery, shirtwaist dress with a
thin belt, Grandpa was wearing slacks and a long-sleeved
shirt
without a sports jacket or tie.
This was informal for them;
A grubby day.

I came across a photograph today.
I was in their kitchen that day.
And as I looked at the photograph,
I remembered the perfumed air,
so sweetened by that apple-noodle pudding.
I'm pretty sure I was on napkin placement patrol.

I came across a photograph today.
Grandma, in huge glove potholders, was smiling at the
camera.
Grandpa had his arms out to her
and was looking down at the heat of the oven – for her, of
course.
"Don't get too close to the oven door, darling.
Whatever, I'm right here behind you."

I came across a photograph today.
Of Grandpa standing right behind Grandma.
He was draped in her apron,
with a dishtowel falling over his belt.
He was right behind her –
A well-oiled machine.

I came across a photograph today,
where Grandma had baked a sweet and tart apple-noodle
pudding.
She cooked it from scratch. She even rolled out her own
noodles.
And Grandpa went to work to make the money to buy the
dough
that Grandma rolled out and cut the noodles for the
pudding
that we all savored, that I can still smell,
where no questions were asked,
as I looked at the photograph that I came across today.

And so I thought, who would have imagined
that stuff like noodle dough and dishtowels falling over
men's belts designated a well-oiled machine.

I came across a photograph today
Where no questions were asked.
These apple-noodle puddings either came out good,
or not.

CHAPTER 5 – SHOOT THE CUPID OR...

Depiction of a downdatee who: is from and stays connected to a substantially lower class than the female.
Protagonist: Jennifer

1. Do you know anyone who stubbornly refused to move up from their financial, political, social station, etc... that no longer served them?

   A. What was your relationship with them?

   B. Did they ever "grow" out of their position?

   C. What was that like for you?

   D. How did that affect your friends and family?

2. Jennifer was somewhat hesitant about going to a single's dance. She pre-judged the group as potentially too conservative and/or too religious.

A. What was your general take on the feel of the group?

B. Would this be a single's dance you might attend? Yes___No___

C. What type of single's events do you/would you attend?

D. How often in a month do you try to meet people to date?

0___

1-3___

4-5___

More___

3. Did you know meeting a significant other is a statistics game? Meaning, the more you mingle, the less you are single. If you checked 0 or 1-3 in 2D, your chances of meeting someone is appreciably lower than those who have checked 4-5, or more. How can you increase this?

4. Are you able to attend a single's event alone?

5. Why do you not get out more often (if you don't)?

6. Are there single's events near you that coordinate interests (for example, a political group, a theatre group, book discussion group, gardening, ballroom dance, sports events groups, and so on...)

    A. Could you create one?

    B. If so, what would you create?

7. People commonly say, "I am not a leader. I couldn't create something like this." I say hogwash to that.

    If you really want to, you could network and get anything going.

    What initial contacts would you call, email, etc... if you had to create a social group?

8. A. The night Jen met Jonathan was a beautiful evening in a perfect setting. Write about how you would have felt that evening.

B. Now, write about how it would have been different if you or Jennifer had met Jon in a crowded, loud setting.

9. A. Think of when you met your present or past significant other. How did the setting contribute to your meeting?

B. What if you had met in a totally different type of setting? How might that have influenced your relationship?

10. Do you think Jonathan ever really settled into Los Angeles, or do you think he just came out to L.A. as a temporary jaunt?

A. How did that affect their relationship?

B. Did you ever date someone who was in your city temporarily? What was that like?

11. You are an angel with a message for Jennifer after Jonathan returned to Alabama. What is your message?

12. This same angel has a message for you!

Dear _____ (your name),

(write your message to yourself)

PART 17
WHOSE BLACK NIGHT?

The reason why God's committee created so many time zones, was to remind us – when we are alone and fast asleep in the black night, there definitely is someone else waking up for school, someone cooking their children lunch, someone going to worship their God, someone coming from not worshiping somebody else's lifestyle, someone confused by their boss, and someone else dressing for a date. We may be fast asleep in the black night, but we are never alone.

PART 18
ANOTHER QUERY

Are you involved with a circle of people
who are the best for your highest self?

How about ten years ago?

PART 19
HERE AND NOW

This is a simple, but great, exercise.

A. At this place in time, write what:

    1. You are seeing in the room you are presently in:

_____

    2. You are hearing right now?

_____

    3. Tasting?

_____

    4. Feeling in, or on, your body?

_____

    5. Smelling?

_____

B. 1. In relation to your significant other, write, in one sentence, what you think of him <u>at this very moment</u>?

    2. In one sentence, how do you feel for him (differentiate think vs. feel for you)?

PART 19

3. In one sentence, what is the most pressing thing you want to tell him right now?

Sometimes everything we are is expressed in the here and now. If you can reduce all complexity to feelings of the here and now, you can learn to ground yourself. "Here and Now" can prove powerful. How simple.

Recreate this exercise whenever you need it. Just ask yourself, "How am I feeling this very moment?"

Then, either "act" on it, or insist upon placing a positive spin on it, and "move on." Those two little words again.

PART 20
LESSONS ON A SUNDAY AFTERNOON

I was parked at a red light and saw a gentleman: East Indian or Pakistani, age about 32, assisting a little girl, about six years old, probably his daughter, across the street.

Normally a fairly busy intersection, the streets were quiet and still this sunny Sunday afternoon. The little girl was on a skateboard, deftly balancing. The man had one hand supporting her back and one hand on her arm. She was remarkably concentrating. He was totally beaming into her six year old *I really must master the skateboard* need.

I watched them approach the curb. He helped her off, picked up the skateboard, applauded her, and smiled. His eyes were gleaming even bigger than her smile.

The little girl got back on the skateboard. They resumed her lesson. Neither of them spoke. It all looked like a bit of a routine. They have done this before.

From a farther vantage point, I could see how much he was also leaning into her, supporting her little body, on all fronts, but not doing it for her. I saw interdependence, allowance, and trust on a skateboard.

Wow, I laughed, driving away, what a great Sunday afternoon lesson.

CHAPTER 6 – SOME DANCING, SOME ROMANCING

Description of a downdatee who: is physically or mentally abusive to the Female.

Protagonist: Regina

1. A. For those of you who have studied dance, music, sports, art, etc… who was your main teacher, mentor, or coach?

What did you think their personal life was like outside the studio, gym, classroom and so forth?

B. How do you think Regina's personal life compared to her professional life?

C. What about you? How does your work or school life appear? How does it compare to your social life?

D. Do you think Regina needed more experience in her work or personal life to feel more stabilized? To a major degree, or not?

E. What about you – where do you need more experience or learning? Work, school, or personal?

F. What is the best way to obtain that learning? (If you read the main text and paid attention to the red flags, you have already begun your personal-life classroom).

2. A. How do you perceive friends and family members who are focused on a talent, art form, or passion, in terms of relationships?

___ Do you think it prepares them for relationships?

___ Do you think it detracts from their learning about relationships?

___ Do you think: This doesn't really apply at all since they are involved in another in-depth learning experience.

Artists take on a slightly different set of responses towards relationships.

B. Explain your response.

3. A. It has been said that people involved in an art form or passion, overall, date down considerably less. Why do you think that is?

B. If you were more involved in a passion or art form, would you date down less?

C. I fully support not over-focusing on significant others. Being involved in activities you treasure helps this. Explain your level of activities/involvement.

4. A. Sometimes, children want to get involved in a talent or passion but their parents do not carry through with their wishes, do not have the funds for learning, and so forth. Where were you regarding this in your childhood?

B. What are your feelings surrounding this issue now, as you reflect?

5. A. Do you know it is NEVER too late to get involved in a talent/passion? You do not have to be great, but you do have to love it.

It has also been noted that one of the greatest detractors for moving on from a downdatee is to dive, head first, into a passion. How has this possibly affected you in the past?

B. What might you be able to dive into to express yourself and deflect from negative relationships?

_____

_____

_____

C. Give me one sentence why you are not looking into this already?

The reason I am not looking into a healthy "deflection" is because_____.

6. Do you think Mark has potential for the change Regina needs and deserves in a relationship?

7. Do you think she over-reacted to Mark's Narcissism? Do you think she under-reacted? Why?

8. What kind of woman could happily co-exist alongside Mark without any problems?

9. Do you know any emotionally abusive men who are not abusive in every situation? (For example, Mark was even-tempered with his son, Ben.) Who is this person and what is his situation?

10. Do you think Benjamin had an inkling his dad was overly demanding with women?

11. Before you read this story with the red flag analysis, would you have thought Mark was abusive or not? (Be honest!)

12. Which red flag of the entire story really hit home with you and why?

13. Look at Red Flag #7. Rewrite the definition of abuse in your own words:

To me abuse means _____.

14. Can you think of anyone in your life–family member, friend, etc. who should buy the main text just to have a better understanding of emotional abuse?

Yes ___ No ___

15. Who is this person / these people?

Perhaps the main text would be a meaningful gift for these people who could use some new insights.

PART 22
A LITTLE ASIAN MYTHOLOGY

There is a charming myth in Japanese mythology about a goddess named Amaterasu.

In this myth, Amaterasu became so upset with the violence around her, that she buried herself deep inside a cave and refused to come out.

This isolation was not good because she took the sun with her inside the cave and there was no sunshine for the rice fields and consequently the people started to go hungry.

The community decided to make much noise but the noise did not lure Amaterasu out of the cave. Then, the community shone a bronze mirror inside the cave, hoping her reflection would lure Amaterasu out. This did not work. Then, a wise man decided to show her a beautifully bejeweled necklace. The gem-filled necklace finally lured her out of the cave with the sun, and once again the beloved rice fields continued to flourish.

This is a charming myth, but you have to ask yourself, do you date down because someone is luring you with a "bejeweled necklace" and nothing else? Do you date for material goods and receive no integrity? If you do, you really need to write about this issue.

PART 23
TARGET

I noticed him staring at me as soon as I arrived in the department. And there he continued – eyeing me through the red bullseye sign at Target. Why is he staring at me so closely?

He was handsome. The minor glimpse I took of him – black cashmere coat, leather gloves.

"Ah–excuse me, ma'am?"

I can't believe it, I thought. *He is going in for the kill at Target, by the socks.*

I quickly scanned the department. There were other sock buyers. I wasn't alone.

I noticed he was holding two pairs of ladies colored tights. *Gimme a break.*

"Yes?" I responded, whilst backing up a little.

"I don't mean to bother you, but which of these tights do you like better? The dark green or the navy blue? I don't really know about this stuff."

"Oh, um, er–the navy blue. It will go with more," I guardedly responded.

"I can see that. Thank you so much. Sorry to bother you," he said, placing the green pair back on the shelf. "Appreciate it."

Then he waved, walked away behind the red bullseye Target sign and vanished somewhere around the oversized brassieres.

Sometimes a rose is a rose is a rose.

PART 24
AN EXERCISE IN SEEING THE POSITIVE

1. If you could rewrite any part of history in the world, what would you rewrite?

2. If you could rewrite any part of your romantic history, what would you rewrite?

3. Yet – what is something positive you learned from the aspect you'd like to rewrite in question two? Please elaborate.

PART 25
CHARACTERISTICS

1. Which of the following characteristics are important to you in a relationship –

    1– very important
    2– fairly important
    3– not important

    Honesty   1___ 2___ 3___
    Communication   1___ 2___ 3___
    Generosity   1___ 2___ 3___
    Friendliness   1___ 2___ 3___
    Responsible   1___ 2___ 3___
    Self-reflective   1___ 2___ 3___
    Sense of humor   1___ 2___ 3___
    Willingness to grow   1___ 2___ 3___
    Has common sense   1___ 2___ 3___
    (Anything else?) _____   1___ 2___ 3___

2. Which of the following characteristics are important for your significant other NOT to have –

    1– very important not to have
    2– fairly important not to have
    3– not very important to me either way

    Lack of kindness   1___ 2___ 3___
    Dishonesty   1___ 2___ 3___
    Non-communicative   1___ 2___ 3___

Very withdrawn	1___	2___	3___
Irresponsible	1___	2___	3___
Will not look at self	1___	2___	3___
Cannot laugh at self	1___	2___	3___
Closed to personal growth	1___	2___	3___
No common sense	1___	2___	3___
(Anything else?) _____	1___	2___	3___

3. Now go back and list all the characteristics in Question One that are very important. List all the characteristics in Question Two that are most important NOT to have. Where does your significant other fit in with these two lists?

PART 26
ART CLASS

On this blank sheet, paste photos or draw pictures of people who have been supportive of you this year.

CHAPTER 7 – GIRL WITH A SILVER SPOON IN HER WALLET

Depiction of a downdatee who: is chronically unemployed, has no aspirations of exceeding minimum wage and/or is financially supported by the female.

Protagonist: Kristina

1. A. Very few citizens of the United States come from such extraordinary family wealth as Kristina. If you did come from such tremendous, old money (that seemed to keep on coming), how would you expose it to your significant others?

___ 1. Keep it very obscured, non-disclosed.

___ 2. Disclose it slowly on a case-by-case basis.

___ 3. Not really care.

___ 4. Be totally open about family wealth.

___ 5. Let everyone know, quickly, who I am and what I come from.

___ 6. Lead most significant others to believe I have much less money than I do.

___ 7. Always present myself as having much money (even when I do not) so as to gather respect.

B. In present day, how do you expose your financial situation? Which of the above fits you most realistically in real time?

1. ___ 2. ___ 3. ___ 4. ___ 5. ___ 6. ___ 7. ___

C. Does this verbal financial positioning work for you?

Yes ___ No ___

Why does it work for you, or, what needs changing?

2. Kristina's driver made the initial call to the therapist for her. Apparently, Mr. and Mrs. Hamilton sent Peter, her driver and assistant, to California with Kris to "look after her." This was based on Kristina's bad decision-making during her senior year at university. She did not seem to oppose the chaperoning.

Was there ever a time in your adult life when you wished someone else would "look after you," or, at least carry the ball for a while?

Women commonly feel this need when they are in the midst of a dating down relationship because downdatees rarely carry their share of the load. On some subtle, or overt, level these men expect everything to be done for them.

Therefore, was there a time when you wished someone would be your personal assistant for a while? Did this time, indeed, have to do with a downdatee or not? Write about it.

3. The downdatee illustrated in the main text's chapter seven was "chronically unemployed."

A. In your own words, why do you think theirs was a dysfunctional situation?

B. What can you look for to prevent this from happening to you?

4. Kristina gave Dario/Paul large sums of money. Do you think she did it because:

___ A. She felt sorry for him.

___ B. She was "buying" him.

___ C. She had never been touched by someone with such an elaborate ruse and he blindsided her.

5. When Kris and Dario met Polly at the mall during Christmas, it seemed as though Polly was starting to be "on" to him, yet, she never said anything to Kristina.

When do you, personally, alert a friend to your instincts? How does this work for you?

6. Kris was really lucky to have a Bob Constantine in her life. How would you have used his services if you were Kris? When, in your life, did you need one of "those"? How could you have avoided that in the first place?

7. I thought Mr. Hamilton did a brilliant job expressing himself after Kristina's graduation. How do you think Dario felt and how do you fantasized it impacted his future goings-on?

8. Which red flag in *Girl With a Silver Spoon in Her Wallet* was the greatest learning experience for you? What can you do to keep this learning experience going?

9. Besides yourself, might any of the red flags in this story apply to anyone you specifically know? Talking to this person about it might be a great deed. Write down exactly what you might like to share with her/him.

CHAPTER 8 – BEWARE THE SHIRTLESS MAN IN JANUARY

Depiction of downdatee who: has potentially dangerous psychosis or psychopathology.

Protagonist: Mimi

1. A. Let's pretend. At the point when Mimi and Mike were living together, you decided to invite them over for dinner. How do you assume an evening like that went?

B. Were you ever in a situation where you had to spend an evening with another couple who were having great problems, or, with whom you disapproved? How did it feel and how did you handle yourself?

C. How do your friends handle themselves when they are with you and a significant other with whom they disapprove?

D. How much would it help your relationship with them if you all talked about their disapproval? What do you think would happen?

2. Red Flag #4 expounds upon Mimi perceiving Mike as "unique" because he threw money out of the car window.

    Was there a time in your life when you thought someone's mental disorder was unique, creative or cute? What happened?

3. Which of the constants from Chapter One apply to this story?

4. How did you feel towards Mimi throughout the story?
    ____ 1. Compassionate
    ____ 2. Angry
    ____ 3. Scared
    ____ 4. Outraged
    ____ 5. Adoration
    ____ 6. Intrigued, but turned off
    ____ 7. Much identification
    ____ 8. Other_____

5. Were you shocked that someone who was so successful as a fashion model, at a young age, could be so blind to relationships?

Yes ___ No ___

(Do you know career or financial success and relationship sophistication have nothing to do with each other?)

6. You might have learned a bit about psychosis or psychopathology from this story. What else did you learn that has nothing to do with mental illness, but does have to do with dating down?

PART 29
WRITING LETTERS

1. Write a short letter to someone you have not thanked enough. (Feel free to send it.)

2. Write a letter to someone who hurt you in the past whereby you never, quite enough, expressed your upset. (This one, readers, does not have to be critical, filled with trendy four-letter attacks, or sickeningly sentimental. The FACTS ALONE are powerful, and probably, long overdue. I do feel hard copies are more impactful than emails. Feel free to send this one too.)

PART 30
A PLAYLETTE FOR YOU

Setting: Beachfront of a large hotel in Maui, as the sun is setting. Lisa, age fifty-nine and very overweight and a little too overdressed for the balmy night, sits on one of the two lounge chairs, takes off her shoes and looks up at the sky. Then, she looks around, scans her surroundings, makes sure nobody is there, and lights up a cigarette.

Eugene, age nineteen, in surfer shorts, carrying a longboard, enters the scene. He drops his surfboard down and wraps a towel around his shorts. He speaks.

EUGENE

Hello. There's no place to sit. Mind? (He says, drying himself)

LISA

(in a thick Brooklyn accent)

If you and your youthful enthusiasm and your six-pack abdomen don't start counseling me about my smoking. Just stay away from my smoking…and that lounge chair is yours for the duration of your surfinghood.

EUGENE

(Laughing under his breath and drying himself off.)
I...um...I just wanted to relax after a long day at sea.

LISA

(She looks at him incredulously.)
Waddya, nuts? Do I look like some three-headed inbred?
You are trying to make yourself out to be some heroic
Merchant marine? Gimme a break. You're some college
boy, on Christmas break, longboarding.

EUGENE

(He looks at her for a few beats.)
Really, ma'am, I just wanted to sit here because all the
other lounge chairs are back at the hotel and my shorts are
wet.

LISA

Wet in the shorts, not behind the ears.

EUGENE

Not particularly.

LISA

So, where do ya go? Brown? Stanford? University of Texas?
Parents mail you here on their hardworking pensions?

EUGENE

Er...no...actually, I'm a local. I'm a waiter at this hotel.
I don't go to college.

LISA

(Sits back.)
Oh.

EUGENE

Are you in from the mainland?

LISA

Where do you think, Gay Paree?

EUGENE

I didn't think anything.

LISA

At least you don't lie.

   (They eye each other.)

I'm from the heart of Brooklyn and my son is as old as you.
He's in the Navy.

EUGENE

Is that right?

LISA

Yeah. He's stationed in a terrorist-laden country. That's why I
took up smoking again.

EUGENE

I'm really sorry. But, I'm not sure your smoking is going to
help the cause. I mean…maybe you could do something
like take up knitting and then send the boys socks or
something.

LISA

You promised you wouldn't bring up my smoking.

EUGENE

If I recall correctly to nine minutes ago, in all due respect, ma'am, I don't believe I promised anyone an everloving thing.

LISA

(Enjoying his moxie.)
Knitting?

EUGENE

Why not? Or surfing.

LISA

(She laughs.)
How the hell do you get up on that thing? Is it about balance or dogged determination?

EUGENE

Both.
(She reaches over and puts out her cigarette.)

EUGENE

Oh, so you stopped smoking?
(They both laugh.)

EUGENE

Are you travelling with someone or, are you alone, Ms...Ms...

LISA

Lisa, and I'm travelling solo.

EUGENE

You aren't wearing a marriage band.

LISA

(She stares at him.)
I told you my son is as old as you.

EUGENE

(He laughs.)
I'm not picking you up. I wouldn't pick up a smoker.
(He laughs.)

But...I was just wondering...see, my dad is travelling alone. Spending the week with me. We were going to go to dinner after my surf. He's also from Brooklyn. Maybe you went to Sunday school or something together. Would you care to join us, Ms. Lisa?

LISA

Why...actually...yes...if it is not too much of an imposition.

EUGENE

Nonsense. The hotel lets me change in the locker rooms. Lobby in a half hour?

LISA

Um...well, yes, fine. Do...do I look okay?
   (She suddenly loses her Brooklyn balsiness and actually comes across a bit vulnerable.)

EUGENE

You look beautiful.
   (He extends his hand. They shake hands.)
Everyone is friendly around here. It's great. Vacationers and staff.

LISA

Yes, sure. Okay–half hour. Oh–what is your name?

EUGENE

(Gathering his stuff.)

I'm Eugene Roman and my dad is Sylvester. Think of any restaurant you wanna go to, Lisa. Dad is totally cool. Later!

(He runs off.)

(Lisa looks back at him. She takes out her compact, powders her nose, applies lipstick and sprays her mouth with a blast of Binaca. Then she takes out her pack of cigarettes, toys with it, and discards it in a nearby trash can. She looks back at the ocean and smiles.)

LISA

Knitting?

(She walks toward the brightly lit hotel.)

PART 31
QUESTIONS TO THE READER REGARDING A PLAYLETTE FOR YOU

(You're not getting off the hook that easily)

1. Believe it or not, we are going to discuss safety. Here goes.

When people travel or are on vacation they somewhat tend to lower their standards.

Lisa maintained safety in this situation because she did not give Eugene her last name or tell him what hotel she is staying in, and, is planning to meet him in a busy hotel lobby.

If she is to maintain this safety level for the remainder of the evening, what other "precautions" must she take?

2. If you travel alone, what safety measures do you exercise?

3. In any of the eight stories from the main text, did any of the gals behave unsafely? Who stands out in your mind, and when?

4. Do you think there is a correlation between dating down and not maintaining safety? Can you explain?

PART 32
MORE SELF EXAMS

Are you involved with a circle of people
who are the best for your highest self?

Are you more tired of this question, or of

the circle of friends who are not best for your highest self?

Be honest.

PART 33
AN EXTREMELY SHORT MOVIELETTE FOR YOU

(Camera opens with an extreme close-up of an electric-orange colored high-top gym shoe. As it pulls back, we see the shoe on the floor of a busy shoe store. Four girlfriends, around twenty years old, are seated nearby.

Four-shot of Annie, Franny, Dani and Hannie.)

ANNIE

You know you want to buy them, Franny.

DANI

I think she just likes the salesman – more than the orange high-tops.

HANNIE

In fact, I think she likes the salesman so much, I think we should all go next door to Gothic Golightly and leave them to their own devices.

PART 33

(The three friends giggle and exit the store. We see
Franny, shocked at their behavior. From her point
of view, we see her eyeing Jim, the salesman. He is
apparently checking her out as well.)

Your Turn – I told you it was extremely short!

1. Use your own paper for this assignment. Finish this movielette with a healthy dialogue between Franny and Jim. (You do not have to understand camera angles, etc... Just write their dialogue.) Feel free to bring the friends back in if you like, but the main thing is Franny and Jim's introductory dialogue.

2. Now, re-write the dialogue "unhealthily." You do not have to be a seasoned writer and remember, nobody is grading you. But, this will be a beneficial exercise to see if you can understand a clean difference between healthy versus unhealthy first hellos. Have fun. Give it a try.

3. What did you learn?

4. What can you apply to yourself?

PART 34
RESPONSE TO CHAPTER NINE CHAPTER 9 IS ENTITLED WHAT HAPPENED TO THE GALS?

1. A. Think about the outcome of these women. Did you expect different endings? Which outcomes surprised you and which ones did not?

- Chapter 1 – ___ Surprised ___ Not surprised
- Chapter 2 – ___ Surprised ___ Not surprised
- Chapter 3 – ___ Surprised ___ Not surprised
- Chapter 4 – ___ Surprised ___ Not surprised
- Chapter 5 – ___ Surprised ___ Not surprised
- Chapter 6 – ___ Surprised ___ Not surprised
- Chapter 7 – ___ Surprised ___ Not surprised
- Chapter 8 – ___ Surprised ___ Not surprised

B. Check the outcome that you least predicted.

2. You can well understand the injurious effects dating down can leave on people, their family, and their friends, sometimes, for years into the future.

Which character in the book do you imagine was most affected by this injury?

3. If she were you, what would you do to heal? (But first you might like to ask, is healing generally possible in YOUR mind? Please don't say no.)

PART 35

FROM THE CLOSING CHAPTER

1. A. Chapter Ten, or the final chapter is called *A Closing Word, or Dating Up from Down*.

   What was the main piece you took away from this chapter?

   B. How would you phrase that to a friend who is presently dating down?

2. Is there a possibility this book and workbook might help them in acquiring some of their very own, necessary insights?

___ Yes

___ No

___ Maybe

___ It is definitely worth a try

___ Yes, and I will ask her (him) if we shouldn't start a dating down support group

PART 36
FIVE THINGS

1. If there are five things you can take away from the entire experience of reading the text, working in the workbook, perhaps starting a dating down discussion group (where you might study a chapter and its red flag per week), what would these five things be?

1. _____

2. _____

3. _____

4. _____

5. _____

2. How are you, ever so slightly, changed by this experience?

3. This is YOUR workbook. What is your particular final word?

PART 37
THE WORKBOOK'S FINAL WORD

This is your final workbook question. You, the reader, and I, the author, are forever joined because (choose only one):

___ I expressed an entire, long-awaited book and workbook for your enjoyment and your growth and you accepted the offering.

___ You have now seen me naked.

And, these are my last workbook comments:

I so wish you a life of UP.

I do wish I could meet all of you. Well...anything is possible.

How did I ever fit in that tub?

~ Thanks for sharing ~

~ Love yourself ~

Visit me at www.DatingDownBook.com

~ Until next time ~

AUTHOR BIO

Carole H. Field is a writer, an international lecturer and a licensed psychotherapist.

She is also a trained ballet dancer and has 4 vocal octaves.

She would also like to make dinner for all her readers but thinks some things might be impossible...maybe.

In the meantime, you can visit her on DatingDownBook.com

Made in the USA
Charleston, SC
19 June 2010